T0381234

# UNSUNG LOVE

DR. STEPHANNIE S. HUEY

*iUniverse books may be ordered through booksellers or by contacting:*

*iUniverse*
*1663 Liberty Drive*
*Bloomington, IN 47403*
*www.iuniverse.com*
*1-800-Authors (1-800-288-4677)*

*ISBN: 978-1-5320-4867-8 (sc)*
*ISBN: 978-1-5320-4868-5 (e)*

*Library of Congress Control Number: 2018905229*

*Print information available on the last page.*

*iUniverse rev. date: 08/08/2018*

# DEDICATION

This book is dedicated to ALL those who have loved with their whole heart, mind, and soul. Love is not lost.

To: Frankie M.

The overseer on earth of my soul.
I am grateful for your spiritual love and support
through this life's journey.

To: My Heavenly Father
Thank you for using your vessel to share your infinite wisdom.
It is my prayer that all who read this divine work
will come to know endless and unconditional love—your love.

# CONTENTS

FOREWORD ................................................................ vii

Introduction ............................................................. ix

1. "A SEASON GONE BY" ................................................. 1
2. "The Forbidden Love" ............................................... 2
3. "Let Go My Heart" ................................................. 3
4. "Untamed" ......................................................... 4
5. "Old School Love" ................................................. 5
6. "Early Morning Embrace" ........................................... 6
7. "Fear To Commit" .................................................. 7
8. "Heart Throb" ..................................................... 8
9. "Anticipation" .................................................... 9
10. "Love's not Wrong" ............................................... 10
11. "Trust Your Gut" ................................................. 11
12. "Opposites Attract" .............................................. 12
13. "Forever" ........................................................ 13
14. "Play Hard-To-Get" ............................................... 14
15. "Being Kicked While Down" ........................................ 15
16. "Foolish Love" ................................................... 16
17. "Tears of the Heart" ............................................. 17
18. "Left Behind" .................................................... 18
19. "The Eye of the Storm" ........................................... 19
20. "Never Alone—Never Forgotten" .................................... 20
21. "The Invisible Made Visible" ..................................... 21
22. "A Saved Sinner's Plea" .......................................... 22
23. "The Right One" .................................................. 23
24. "Outer Body Experience" .......................................... 24
25. "Break the Spell" ................................................ 25
26. "Prime Time" ..................................................... 26
27. "Childhood Scars Disappear" ...................................... 27
28. "Soul Crying" .................................................... 28
29. "A Treasure from Heaven" ......................................... 29

30. "Generational Curse" ..................................................30
31. "Will He Recognize Me?" ...........................................31
32. "Weirdness" ............................................................32
33. "A Neighborhood Disappeared" ................................33
34. "Souls Don't Die" ....................................................34
35. "God's Justice Is Not Blind" .....................................35
36. "Look Within" .........................................................36
37. "Stillness" ..............................................................37
38. "Life Is an Art" ........................................................38
39. "Don't Go" ..............................................................39
40. "Detours of Life" .....................................................40
41. "The Over Rider" .....................................................41
42. "Artificial Tears" ......................................................42
43. "Guard Your Heart" .................................................43
44. "My Story Is Not Over" ............................................44
45. "Citizenship" ...........................................................45
46. "Faith Activates God" ...............................................46
47. "A Fill-In" ................................................................47
48. "Crossing the Centuries" ..........................................48
49. "No More Battles" ....................................................49
50. "Unknown Lover" .....................................................50
51. "Under His Shadow" .................................................51
52. "Create Your Own" ...................................................52
53. "Free Spirit" ............................................................53
54. "Portrait of Life" ......................................................54
55. "Power to Be" ..........................................................55
56. "A Tribute to the Greatest" .......................................56
57. "A Soul's Desire" ......................................................57
58. "The Other Wooer" ...................................................58
59. "Give Love a Chance" ...............................................59
60. "Time to Move On" ...................................................60
61. "Sustainable Love" ...................................................61
62. "Unmeasurable" .......................................................62
63. "Exclusive Rights, ....................................................63
64. "A Strong Presence" .................................................64
65. "Hereafter" ..............................................................65
66. "Hidden Places" .......................................................66
67. "Messages From Afar" ..............................................67
68. "Can't Travel Backwards" ..........................................68
69. "Partners for Life" ....................................................69
70. "No Imaginary Friend" ..............................................70

# FOREWORD

The writings/poems that Dr. Stephannie S. Huey has so patiently and carefully penned have been inspired by the Holy Spirit that dwells within her being. It is no doubt that she has been touched with a special anointing and giving a gift from the Heavenly Father to spread and promote a divine message to reach all mankind. She shares her poems and life experiences with many as a way to encourage hope, peace, joy, and love.

Her two previous books, *Poetry from the Heavens—Living Out Loud for Jesus,* and *Legacy of Life—"Brava",* were written under the power on the Holy Spirit and has been shared to many as an inspiring and lifting testimony of how God can save and provide a safe place of salvation. She has shared many copies with her colleagues and they have expressed the blessing that they experienced just by reading the authentic words enumerated throughout her works.

I believe that many will receive blessings and eternal comfort from reading the Holy inspired words of the artistically penned poetry. I truly believe that the poems will minister to a variety of human life experiences.

All my life I have watched and admired my mother, Dr. Stephannie S. Huey, as a pastor, teacher and mentor. She has touched many lives with her kindness, generosity, and unceasing love. I fully and wholeheartedly endorse all of her works that I know are inspired the Holy Trinity.

This book is a product of hard work, long hours, many prayers, and sharing back in the day stories. I pray that all of the books that my mother has written will be widely distributed around the world. So, that many can receive a blessing and even discover a spiritual break through that will draw many to know the Father, Jesus Christ, and the Holy Spirit.

*~Taneshia M. Jones, MBA~*

# INTRODUCTION

I give all the honor and praise to my Lord and Savior Jesus Christ, for using His humble servant to display His good works in creating the inspired words of this book. Only through life's experiences, could produce the contents of this spiritual journey. Every trial, heartache, misstep in life, and getting back up again has been imprinted on the poems of this book.

For such a time as this, the Father prepared me to leave another eternal legacy so that all can be saved and have hope. Grant you this was not an easy task, but it has been worth the time and effort devoted to share some of my profound feelings and allow others into my world. This manuscript did not take years to write—only one really. It was easy to let the Father's Words flow on the pages. I just was an instrument doing the typing.

As I began writing poetry again, I realized that God had planted a seed inside of me from the beginning of my existence. And, His timing caused the seed to germinate and bring forth the three masterpieces: *Poetry from the Heavens—Living Out Loud for Jesus, Legacy of Life—"Brava", and Unsung Love.*

In this book, God has revealed that true love endures and conquers much—pain, suffering, homelessness, and hides a multitude of impurities. As you explore each poem, you will encounter laughter, sorrow, recovery, and survival. I want you to find your blessings as you share the bliss of God's creation in me to pen every poem.

Ambassador for Christ,
Dr. Stephannie S. Huey

# "A SEASON GONE BY"

I traveled many miles to look you in the eyes,
Just to look upon your encouraging smile,
I could always depend on you to energize my wavering soul,
From the storms of life that seems to beat unceasingly like rigid cold,
But, our spirits could not connect due to a season gone by,

Years of nurturing and caring for that moment to walk side by side,
Appears to have faded in the distance time thrashing tide,
Though our lives have taken different paths, the love will always last,
Now, enjoy your life with a blast,
For, we were but for a season gone by,

Yes, it is hard to let go, but the memories will linger,
As each year tick away, and there is only a glimmer,
Soon we'll only hope to remember, moments in each other's presence,
While traveling across this vast universe, in God's omnipresence,
Looking backwards on a season gone by,

No, we did not get to dance under the stars,
Or, stroll side by side and laugh in the park,
But, for a moment in time, I enjoyed your smile,
That allowed me to travel for miles and miles,
So, good bye to a season gone by,

Now, it is time for you to soar high into the sky,
While keeping your eyes on the prize and telling life to standby,
And, watch you mesmerize the crowd with your godly talent,
As, I watch from afar in silent,
For it was a season gone by,

# "THE FORBIDDEN LOVE"

The forbidden love that is not spoken,
Hiding in the shadows with hearts broken,
Yearning each day to touch the core of each other's essence,
But, never feeling your lover's presence,

A love that defies society's standards,
That walks upright in the face of judging bystanders,
Without shame or disgrace,
Standing strong with God's amazing grace,

Oh, how they long to shout their love from the mountaintop,
And, express it as the morning glistening dew drops,
Their love erupts like a volcano's hot lava,
Devoid of all street drama,

Why must the forbidden love die in silence?
Because mankind sits in mindless darkness,
To scorn the purity of sweet and innocent lovers,
Who are joined as soulmates as time rediscover,

A forbidden love standing in the midst of scorn,
And, not willing to conform,
But, embracing each moment of everlasting ecstasy,
For true love will never deny its destiny,

Now, ponder no longer over set rituals,
Yet, harness the power of universal blissfulness,
Openly confessing your love to the entire world,
And, no longer a forbidden love to be unobserved,

# "LET GO MY HEART"

A captured heart suspended in subliminal hypnoses,
Like Rip Van Winkle asleep in an enchanted unconsciousness,
To escape the worldly hideous noises,
As the life sustaining vessel throbs with faintness,

I search endlessly for unwavering serenity,
While perched atop of life's uncertainty,
As I pray for God's beckoning eternity,
Let go my heart to be ravished in blissful gaiety,

Unlock the chains that binds my heart of gold,
So, that another prospective suitor can warm me from the cold,
And, restore that lost hope that years of imprisonment stole,
That kept me bound from a touch of one's love so bold,

Oh, how one touch can electrify,
The dormant cells lying unsolidified,
As I soar blindly through an enchantment mystified,
Let go my heart from being paralyzed,

A heart engulfed in a loveless fortress,
Like a zombie moving as a tortoise,
I must rebuild a new life to awaken a beautiful chorus,
To exit with a song of perfect performance,

Take a roll call from the Sentinels,
As they were posted around the precious jewel,
Did they guard your heart raised on a pedestal?
Yes. And, demanded, let go the heart it's not accessible,

# "UNTAMED"

Once upon a time, a soul descended to earth untamed,
Unlogged from its heavenly celestial frame,
To become entangled in a brand-new ballgame,
And playing on a field with no shame,

Always striving to hit a home run,
While holding the bat in perfect form,
Never relinquishing control as you perform,
Just standing firmly at home plate transformed,

Until one day strolled along the beach front,
A tall gladiator strong and mighty that made you grunt.
That shifted your ice cap as he stepped to confront,
He unleashed an all-points bulletin woman hunt,

A gladiator soft spoken with charisma,
Enough to dismantle the untamed woman's stigma,
And, his alluring aroma of vanilla,
A perfect gentleman—not a gorilla,

With no tactical plan of defense,
The untamed woman can't jump across the fence,
But, must submit to the gladiator with no pretense,
A woman tamed with love so intense,

Emerging deeply in the gladiator's pulsating embrace,
Which banished all fears of rejection—let's celebrate,
No more running—no more hiding—no more masquerading,
A woman tamed by two souls interfacing,

# "OLD SCHOOL LOVE"

Let a man open doors and pull out chairs,
Even wash and comb your hair,
And, welcome you home with a tub of warm bubbles,
While washing your back as you cuddle,
Old school love verses 21st Century swindle,

Watch him mix and whip up a meal,
Go ahead stroke his ego, make a big deal,
What do you say when a man massages the back of your heels?
And, swoop you off your feet like a man of steel,
Old school love verses 21st Century wheeling and dealing,

No cell phone or texting an unknown party,
Never arriving late or tardy,
But, always hating to depart,
Building a relationship strong with an armed guard,
Old school love verses 21st Century multiparty,

A real man picking up the dinner tab,
And, stepping up to flag down a cab,
He's not a cad.
Who likes to grab,
Old school love verses 21st Century dip and dab,

While the flames of intimacy are rising like fireworks,
Your man ignites teamwork,
No selfish gratification or being out of work,
Forever ready to lay the groundwork,
Old school love verses 21st Century guesswork,

# "EARLY MORNING EMBRACE"

The years went flying by leaving remanence of memories,
Of their warm an alluring early morning embrace,
As the alarm clock kept sounding,
You could hear only two hearts pounding,
From the others early morning embrace,

Then came silence over the lonely years,
And, a brisk chilling coldness that brought fears,
That filled the emptiness of a damp room,
No more warmth only sadness and gloom,
Because the two hearts ceasing to embrace,

A love that was meant to last forever,
Got beaten by the storms of life oppressor,
Which scattered love like a shipwreck,
And, left behind only baggage in the cargo deck,
That splintered the sweet loving embrace,

Now, the lovers have permanently departed,
With no hope of love ever being restarted,
One married to settle for a substitute,
The other just hibernated in solitude,
Barely remembering their forging embrace,

Father time will one day arrive,
To capture the two lovers' souls that were deprived,
And, just maybe, time will stand still,
For one last glance before paying the final bill,
Then, imprint an eternal early morning embrace,

# "FEAR TO COMMIT"

I see you running that marathon,
Bobbing and weaving like Megatron,
Trying to encase your heart in a wall of ton,
To avoid being on a chess board like a pond,

Yes, you even invested in a hover board,
Trying be like the Jettison—so feet won't touch the floor,
Your homeboys tease—watch the proverbial sword,
So, you vanish like smoke, and cut the cord,

Slow down my brother before you take a spill,
Stop ducking and dodging 24/7—stop to build,
A permanent relationship and be real,
Then, rare back on easy street and chill,

Put down the streets and stop slanging,
It's time to pace yourself—no more banging,
And, serve notice to all outside females—you aren't hanging,
Because you discarded old junk in the trunk clanging,

Open your intellect to the possibilities of success,
And, with a good woman you can be your best,
Just open your heart and God will do the rest,
To a new day of prime-time blissfulness,

Now, awaken to a new dawn of manhood—submit,
To invest in one woman, that won't quit,
See, your love is like a hand in a glove—that fit,
No more fears, it's time to commit,

# "HEART THROB"

Let's walk along the beach hand in hand,
Watching the sunset along the horizon,
As we stroll through life playing on the big screen,
Like the main characters in a Broadway scene,
We became each other's heart throb holding beam,

Though we have been knocked down and bounced around,
Often leveled completely to the hard ground,
Sometimes ridiculed and even ostracized,
But, we never lost our identity while being scandalized,
We beat as one heart throb uncompromised,

Now, we wake each day strong in each other's arms,
There is nothing this earth can do to press alarms,
Yes, we've put on our full breastplate of protection,
To sustain us from any worldly rejection,
We stand untied one heart throb reflection,

In battle we stand against the bellowing winds attack,
Standing strong—because God's got our backs,
Ready to present a strong frontal assault,
And, keeping the strong man from throwing us to the asphalt,
Our heart throb is built like a vault,

It's time to serve notice on all the haters,
Don't enter the no-fly zone—we aren't players,
We've weathered many years in the universe,
In full driving mode—not thrusted in reverse,
Two hearts—but one heart throb to converse,

# "ANTICIPATION"

I smell your essence everywhere in the air,
I feel your breath like wings of doves so fair,
I taste the sweetness of your ruby lips,
I hear your voice blowing like the summer breeze,
I anticipate your touch moving over me,

O, what ecstasy your presence brings,
It's a mystery of delight unfolding,
That tingles my throat like sweet wine,
Causing electrifying charges down my spine,
And, elevating me to cloud nine,

Help!!!!! You are all mine,
And, it's divine,
This's not a fantasy,
Nor is it vanity,
I just anticipate our intensity,

Our love is like the sweet nectar of a flower,
That burst open every minute of an hour,
Like time on a clock—going around and around,
Wow, you have broken my barriers down,
Anticipation, I feel like royalty with a crown,

Who say love never returns,
Sometimes you just have to wait your turn,
And, let your heart do the listening,
Don't get on any dating sites
Thank you Father for your spiritual divine sight,

# "LOVE'S NOT WRONG"

You heard that song,
"If loving you is wrong"
I don't want to be right,
Because having you in my life,
Makes me feel out of sight,

Then, that cliché,
"Age is but a number"
Let the whole world grumble,
There's no shame in our game,
We don't seek the world's fame,

Solid as a rock,
"No one night stand"
Will land you a true-blue man,
But, there might be an exception to the rule,
If, you know how to groove,

Listen,
"It's not who you meet"
It's when you meet to bring down defeat,
Remember, timing is everything,
To keep lovers exploring,

Have you heard?
"Actions speak louder than words"
Let's keep it moving like big bird,
No actions send up a big flag,
Which causes one to be red tag,

# "TRUST YOUR GUT"

Trust your gut about that special person,
And, shut the outside noises lurking,
To avoid the talking heads of destruction,
That will destroy your physical love connection,

You're drawn to each other day and night,
It's like a griddle pulling you guys tight,
As dreams of each creeps in one's subconscious,
Engulfing your minds in total solace,

Don't be so calculating,
Ignite a flame of trust like comets falling,
Yes, boldly step out on the wild side of spontaneity,
And, experience virtual reality,

Playing the waiting game isn't cool,
Why wait for days to see them again—being a fool,
Or, delaying sending that text message,
Go ahead, trust your gut—have courage,

Stop treating your life like emergency brakes,
It's okay if you make mistakes,
Let's stop driving a Pinto in the slow lane,
And, invest in a classy BMW that glides like a plane,

Now, reel in that special someone like a fish on a hook,
Let true love spring up like a fresh mountain brook,
You've found that special someone when you least expect,
It's time to block the other prospects,

# "OPPOSITES ATTRACT"

It's being known that opposites attract,
Let's test the theory to see if it's on track,
Before you buy into the cliché—opposites attract,
Opposites can be good together, explore the fact,

Take preacher kids (PK)
Are said to be bad and good,
But, seemed to entice all kind of crude,
The good girls like bad boys in the hood,

The Beauty and the Beast, that's unattractiveness,
Or, can the Beauty calm the fiery Beast's brittleness?
That will reinforce lovingkindness,
And, stimulate a sense of righteousness,

What say an aristocrat marrying a commoner?
That's a big difference between two partners,
Is it a recipe for everlasting lovers?
Or, a storyline for the moviegoers,

Now, here's a tip—similarities don't mix,
Couples whose personalities reflects isn't a fix,
There's no excitement—the two can't click,
Where's the intimacy switch?

The moral of the story—opposites attract,
That's a proven scientific fact,
So, says the psychologist the brainy acts,
To keep a smooth relationship on track,

# "FOREVER"

I don't know when I will see you again,
But, I know this love I have will linger within,
I will carry you in my heart to the very end,
No, this kind of love won't bend,

Though, we never touched that inner core,
We've being on a distant shore,
Drifting in two ships without an oar,
Moving like a tidal wave going ashore,

It seems you've ditch me all day long,
And, now I'm stranded home alone,
No texting, twitting, or a call on the cell phone,
It is what it is—you've gone,

Take the memories that we've accumulated,
Maybe, one thought will leave you stimulated,
To remember, our kind of love can't be duplicated,
Because, we were never regulated,

Time won't stand still,
To allow love to build,
And, I can't travel in my time machine at will,
Back to the innocent moment on the hill,

So, until the lighthouse shines to lead us again,
To reunite on the same plane,
I pray our souls will never be in pain,
For, our love was never in vain,

# "PLAY HARD-TO-GET"

Is it true, whoever cares less wins?
So, love is reduced to a game blowing in the winds,
Does it work in your favor to care less?
Lovers have stopped trying to impress,

Can the less interested you play on the acting stage?
Promote a more intriguing and luring cage,
Why play hard to get?
Just to send another to break out in a cold sweat,

What? Being emotionally driven make you care more?
Because, you don't want to be a bore,
Will you then cave into your partner's desires?
And, give up game playing that extinguish fires,

What does it matter who makes the first move?
All is fair in love that grooves,
Is it possible, we both are mutually connected in the zone?
Let's become each other's clone,

Who does it benefit?
Playing hard to get,
Wouldn't it be easier just to submit?
And, enjoy each other's laughter and wit,

Is it time to tear the player's page out your book?
So, you can establish love running like a spring brook,
Really? Whoever cares less wins?
It's time to drop this cliché in the trash bin,

# "BEING KICKED WHILE DOWN"

Yes, you're kicked while down,
But, you can rise from the ground,
Even though your love ones are not around,
To lend you a helping hand to rebound,

It's time to search for strength within,
God's protection helps you withstand the bend,
God promised to be with you to the end,
God's love will never rescind,

Time has come to stop the eternal bleeding,
Look to the abundant love within for re-seeding,
You must stop going through life speeding,
Push pause—not allow your heart to keep leading,

Life's spinning out of control,
What happened to your goal?
It's like you've traveled to the North Pole,
Put your life on emergency patrol,

Okay, so you've suffered great pain,
And, it appears you're living in vain,
As you watch the world's greedy gain,
It's a world gone insane,

Grab hold to God's unchanging hand,
For His love will take a grandstand,
Bounce back like a rubber band,
Refuse to be kicked down—now stand,

# "FOOLISH LOVE"

Let me tell you a story of foolish lovers,
Entangled with storm clouds of heartache that hovered,
That poured much distance between the two lovers,
One took cover and the other burnt rubber,

As the years ticked away sounding like Old Father time,
The two lovers succumbed to societal judging mind,
And, dismissed their love sent from Heaven above,
To fit into a fake illusion of an earthly club,

Now, their love has widened as the east from the west,
There was no dam to engulf the love in their breast,
The fiery love that burned everlasting—extinguished,
With a tidal wave that—diminished,

One holding on to yesterday's memories,
While the other moved on, to write other stories,
Have the chapters of their book come to an end?
Oh, there are two lovers that did not win,

Two hearts afraid to explore,
Just closed the door,
Of endless possibilities that could flow,
And, stopped the love before it could grow,

Two lovers caught in a stereotype,
While society perpetrate hype,
Society's standards sealed the lovers' plight,
Their love no longer shine bright,

Now, the sunset brings darkness,
The stars no longer twinkle in their eyes,
And, the moon hides behind the clouds,
Was it foolish love—engulfed in a shroud?

# "TEARS OF THE HEART"

It's like Niagara Falls that flows and flows.
Tears of the heart just blows and blows.
It's like an oil rig just being tapped.
Tears of the heart fell in a wormhole trap.

It's like a volcano of dynamite.
To find your heart emerged in the twilight.
As you woke with a pillow wet.
Tears from your heart—not sweat.

Did a giant boulder wipe out your lucidity?
To destroy your sanity.
Call the U.S. Calvary.
Let's petition for amnesty.

It's like one crack in Aksomobo Dam.
Little Po Peep couldn't save the lamb.
It's like a herd of stallions running on the beach.
Tears of the heart suffers a stampede breach.

It's like jumping out of a Kitty Hawk's plane
And landing without a parachute in the Great Plains.
It's like throwing a boomerang.
Tears of the heart took your survival game.

It's like a building consumed in flames.
You made your own tears—who can you blame?
It's like the Titanic capsizing.
Guess what, tears of the heart are traumatizing.

# "LEFT BEHIND"

There were seven bound together,
Stronger than a speeding train battery,
Invincible to earthly catastrophe,
And, defying living in poverty,

The seven vowed to love and protect,
They never allowed worldly fame to distract,
Since, separation was not an option,
Their mother instilled a firm foundation,

The seven grew wiser and older,
Explorers of life's amenities like voyagers,
Vessels with knowledge to share,
If casted out to sea—strong winds they would bare,

The woes of life imposed on the seven's sanctuary,
The Grim Reaper of calamities changed their planetary,
Fighters for all humanity—that's the seven,
Yes, unsung heroes—the seven sent from Heaven,

Now, only two remain from the seven,
Yes, five dreamers are in Heaven,
The two that be—are praying with glee,
That the seven will reunite—it's God's decree,

So, the two await the great reunion,
They're overcomers of grief—not superhuman,
Just believers of the Heavenly Father's communion,
The two are not left behind—they'll reign in salvation.

# "THE EYE OF THE STORM"

Swept into the eye of the storm's fiery,
Like a funnel tornado swirling around atop of a tree,
Then, ejecting you as in a fighter jet,
There's no parachute—so, you fret.

Weatherman predicted turbulence and high winds,
To destroy your outer shell—with a cotton gin,
Hold onto His unchanging hand,
God's love will be your rubber band.

Tick tock—the clock has not chimed,
Believe it or not—it's not your time,
Roll back the dark clouds of misery,
Michael and Gabriel just flew in to dispel trickery,

Marching to a new song like the Cherubim,
Dancing around the throne like the Seraphim,
Put on the whole armor—breast plate of righteousness,
To deflect the eye of the storm's recklessness,

Now, spring up with deliverance,
All hail, no more wandering in the wilderness,
For, you were lost in the eye of the storm,
But, God stretched forth love as a healing balm,

# "NEVER ALONE—NEVER FORGOTTEN"

Lo, my spirit once like an oasis,
Drying up in a dark deserted abyss,
Thirsting after one drink of life,
To overcome the surmounting torn rife,

Oh, the loneliness of human companionship,
That leaves me like drift wood of a deserted ship,
And, whose soul is likened to a pin pong ball,
Bouncing around the universal wall,

No place to call home—no lioness den,
Like a tumble weed blowing in the wind,
Forgotten by all whose life you touched,
Now, standing close to the edge of the porch,

Where is your safety net?
Let, a shining knight fly in a private jet,
To swift you away to Mount Zion,
Restoring your soul from a life of crying,

Hear ye, hear ye, the bell does not tow,
Come nestle under God's umbrella,
Never alone—never forgotten,
Living in the Paradise garden,

In God's loving pavilion,
Surrounded by people of billions,
Never alone—never forgotten,
Welcome home, to rest on the clouds of cotton,

# "THE INVISIBLE MADE VISIBLE"

The invisible made visible for all mankind,
To have and to hold the heavens and the earth that twain,
Creating righteous souls to rest in the final great eon,
Dispelling sun, darkness, pain, in the break of dawn,

God created man from invisible and from visible,
From the dust of nature spawn man's divisible,
Which will lead to both death and life,
By love and forgiveness—God saved Eva the wife,

Yes, man is the second angel placed on earth,
With honor, greatness, and glory implanted at birth,
True love appointed man ruler with wisdom,
Over the east, west, north and south kingdom,

The invisible made visible the heavens to see,
The angels singing songs of victory across the vast sea,
As Adam and Eva reside in Paradise,
Genesis told the story of their sacrifice,

Seeing the Lord's perfect compass that has no end,
Who can make Old man time never spend?
Only the invisible made visible controls destiny,
There's no entry to Heaven because of one's pedigree.

Invisible made visible knows no respective of person,
The redeemer of the just and unjust issue out proportions,
Each soul is judged by the pureness of heart,
Don't let your sins keep you apart?

# "A SAVED SINNER'S PLEA"

Before that final curtain goes down,
Hear a saved sinner's plea from the ground,
Set a captive soul free that's been unfairly bound,
From a life of untold misery with a jewel crown.

They placed a crown of thorns on Jesus' head,
Then, crucified our Lord and laid him on a stone bed,
He died to save a sinner like you and me—just to wed,
And, invite us as His bride to the God head.

Oh, saved sinner—your pain can't compare,
To the bloody stripes Jesus had to bare,
Or, the public humiliation with no one to care,
Nor, the vinegar and gall did you share.

The prize of salvation was bought with a price,
Of a non-sinner's life—they roll dice,
And, laid open His flesh with whips of chains that splice,
While, His friend denied Him thrice.

Now, comes the saved sinner's reward,
To reign for all eternity—cutting life's dying chord,
Serve notice to all—shed misery—jump on board,
Yes, the bridegroom is coming with the divine chessboard.

Stop the presses, the internet, twitter, cyberspace,
Look who's riding the clouds—with His amazing grace,
Hear the trumpets announce Jesus' shining face,
He answers the saved sinner's plea—with a strong embrace.

# "THE RIGHT ONE"

A substitute can't compare to what's real,
The wrong one just can't fill the bill,
Going through the motions of caring,
All the time wishing the special one start sharing,

Boxed into a tunnel of upside down emotions,
Trying to find an exit to escape the commotion,
Heart screaming—let me off this roller coaster,
Where is the right one—on loves wanted poster?

Upload time—post wanted signs,
Hey, anyone seen that right one of mine,
Put an ad in the classified section,
Proclaim, your lover missing in action,

Then, wave down a taxi cab,
Beep, beep, do a drive-by grab,
Haul that right one home in handcuffs,
Announce, here's the sheriff no cream puff,

Put the spotlight on high beam,
Tell the lover don't destroy your dreams,
Leave the drama out of the house,
Can't you see we're the right spouse?

Now, build our relationship on a mountaintop,
So, all the world eyes can spin and pop,
Two soulmates breaking through road blocks,
The right one breeds good stock,

No more searching around the block,
Because, the right one cleaned your clock,
Hickory, hickory tick tock,
Soulmates interlock,

# "OUTER BODY EXPERIENCE"

Outer body, outer mind,
It felt like one running out of time,
While looking back at a lifeless body,
Wandering where was everybody,

No lover to mourn at your departure,
No lover to wipe your last tears as you're raptured,
No lover to behold your staring glance,
Or, to say this is not the last dance,

As your spirit hover above,
You think, who will handle you with velvet gloves?
Since you spent your life in blind love,
Where, oh where is your beloved?

Ascending farther and farther to that opened door,
A white light beckons you more,
As you watch the doctors try to restore,
On wings of a dove—you fly away to amour,

Slipping away in everlasting sleep,
With a smile of glee—sadness never to repeat,
It's like butterflies that leap,
And, your reward you'll reap,

Outer sight, outer mind,
There's no earthly love to bind,
The world was unkind,
Yes, you've run out of time,

# "BREAK THE SPELL"

Unquiet love spell gripped your soul,
Pushing hard to break through the icy cold,
To thaw a heart like Antarctica,
And, warm you with heat from Africa,

Love spell—knock down the wall gigantic,
Enchant your heart with a prince romantic,
Who road in on a lighten bolt flashing,
Sweeping you up with loving arms dashing,

Can't you see yourself hopping like a bunny rabbit?
Hey, prince charming—case the love spell—let's cohabit,
Let a spring broke flow 'til your eyes twinkle,
Like the flaws of a diamond that sparkle,

No whip bam—see you later alligator,
Genie, case the spell—put the heart on a defibrillator,
Watch prince charming spend you like an oscillator,
'Til you're put on a respirator,

You spent endless years in a deep well,
Crawling through life like a snail,
Now, an angelical host bid sadness farewell,
And, waved the magic wand—breaking the spell,

# "PRIME TIME"

You've been standing in the shadows,
Waiting for a chance to go prime time,
Look at opportunity knocking,
So, your haters can stop blocking,
It's prime time you're rocking,

You working hard at your grind,
With one goal in mind,
Reading life's playbook behind the line,
Not afraid to break negativity's bind,
Just keeping it 100—moving like a tall pine,

One, two, three—what can you do for me?
Get off of me—you're like a flee,
Don't try to attached yourself to me,
When you've been an absentee,
Yeah, it's prime time—whoopee,

Yep, money ran out, no place to sleep,
You like Little Bo Peep, who lost her sheep,
No friends around to see you weep,
Couldn't hear a peep—beep, beep,
Not even the buzzing of a bumble bee,

Oh, the social media network,
Went on a frenzy blasting your business,
Put it on twitter with a quickness,
Did you hear—prime time causes dizziness,
No. But, did you hear laziness causes paralysis?

Hey, got a call from major TV stations,
To watch your dual-threat sensations,
Move to right—move to left—what's your location?
Its prime time—formation,
Check it out—feel the vibrations,

# "CHILDHOOD SCARS DISAPPEAR"

Today, is a new day, my dear,
When childhood scars disappear,
Scars that stemmed from beatings to the rear,
Scars of teeth prints inflected by grandmother, Mud Dear,

Yes, even scars, mother landed with a thick strap,
Left scars seen and unseen like a steel trap,
Martial scars can blow one's mind—to snap,
But, verbal scars are the worst kind—of crap,

My body looked brand new,
Could it be the Shea butter hue?
Or, the baby oil that covers like honey dew,
Wow! I'm using morning dew like shampoo?

Years of abuse brought battle scars,
And, I hid tears—masking my fears,
Just moving through life—with no one to cheer,
Vowing never to give up—stayed focused on my career,

Surprised, by the illuminated skin like rays from the sun,
Skin appearing ever so sweet like a red juicy plum,
Rejoicing! While getting spiritually rubbed with a healing balm,
Now, I'm anew in God's healing palm,

I've shredded the old skin of burden and abuse,
And, became a new creature with a blood transfuse,
I'll never again go through life getting misused,
Now, Jesus fit me with brand new shoes,

I was once lost in an empty space,
With childhood scars staining my face,
I felt like a stranger in this earthly place,
Hurray! Childhood scars disappeared by God's amazing grace,

# "SOUL CRYING"

I had an experience that knocked me down,
All I could do was fall hopeless to the ground,
And, while on the ground, I sunk further and further,
For, my soul cried out—I loss my big brother,

I felt a stillness in my soul,
As though—my blood had turned icy cold,
What happened that day? I cannot say,
All I knew that he and I will never play,

I hold memories of us playing cards,
Never, in this life did I phantom us being apart,
We took classes together at Miles College,
He had my back in World History seeking knowledge,

Because, I was good in Algebra,
I said come on brother—have courage,
I got you—don't sweat,
We can pass—I promise you that,

One day, while at Miles College,
On a clear fall sunny day,
We sat on a bench, and he saw me crying,
He said—you're not a little girl anymore—start flying,

Today, when the darkness come,
I remember his words that plays like a song,
Then, I brush off life's heavy burdens,
And, rise like a Phoenix and start flying,

I will rise, I will rise,
Because, one day I will look him in the eyes,
I'll join him by and by,
Then, my soul will never cry,

# "A TREASURE FROM HEAVEN"

Some people wish for gold and silver,
To possess precious gems that make you quiver,
And, boast about abundance of houses and land,
While, spinning life marching to a one man's band,

But, as for me, I rather have one treasure,
And, not living a life in a hot cooking pressure,
A treasure not formed by earthly trinkets,
Nor, surrounded with pretending bigots,

I've been blessed with a treasure from heaven,
Who's a friend twenty-four seven,
A priceless jewel, with her own story untold,
She is strong—beautiful and bold,

Mirror, mirror on the celestial wall, look at little Buff,
Dispatched to me as a true angel from Heaven's gulf,
Into my life with unconditional love she brought,
And, not afraid—of the many battles she fought,

She is the treasure that brighten my vessel,
I didn't have to settle for life little pebbles,
And, no need for the artificial glitter,
I've been blessed with a spiritual daughter,

I can endure being earthly poor,
As long as, I'm tied to God's richly core,
To receive blessings and treasures He bestowed,
Treasures from Heaven—my baby girl God sowed,

Olé to Taneshia

# "GENERATIONAL CURSE"

I've done my research on the generational curse,
It's handed down through the female purse,
What do you mean—the female purse?
The place like a kangaroo's baby is nursed,

Exodus 20:5, sins of the father is visited on the child,
When sin travel through the third and fourth generations,
Point in case, grandmother, mother, daughter, granddaughter,
This is how the generational curse is handed down by the Father,

The grandmother had a sinful lifestyle,
And, imputed her sins on the female child,
Causing generations of children to be beguiled,
And, living their lives full of hostile,

Yep, it's the sins of the ancestors,
That started the generational disasters,
And, forced them to roam forty years in the wilderness,
Because, they committed the same sins as their ancestors,

What's the cure for the generational curse?
Grandmother didn't repent,
Mother was saddened and bent,
Along came the third generation—very discontent,

The third-generation daughter read Judges 3:9,
To break the generational curse that bind,
Then, she read 2 Corinthians 5:17,
The Word make Christians new creatures—like oil sheen,

To cure a generational curse—you must repent,
So, fall on your knees, fast, and reverence Lent,
God's grace and love last a thousand times—like cement,
In Jesus' name you're no longer living in torment,

# "WILL HE RECOGNIZE ME?"

We were formed in the image of purity,
Fashioned from a Tabula Rasa,
Before being infected by worldly influences,
That transformed a beautiful vessel—now burned with stains,
Yes, we were born into sin full of pain,

Oh, Father, will you recognize me?
Your perfect creation who was full of love,
Who you sent from heaven above,
Now, exist with insides marred—like railroad tracks,
For, earthly troubles nailed my soul with thumb tacks,

Father, Father, will you recognize me?
For, the cruelty of mankind has tarnished my holy being,
They've woven ugliness 'til their love appears as swine,
Mankind rejected the love in my heart—so I erected stop signs,
How can you recognize my persona?

When I've been severely tarnished,
After swinging on a tie rope of life without a hornist,
Yes, foolishly, I made regrettable mistakes,
And, I fell in a barrow filled with viper snakes,
Then, I became injected with man's poisonous lies,

Father, how will you recognize me?
My soul's being torn by the blistering storm,
Often battered like a ship wreck out at sea,
How will you recognize me?
For, I have lost my ability to see,

Oh, my child, I am Alpha and Omega,
Did I not call into existence the universe?
And, created the heavens and the earth,
I hold the winds in my hands—and calm raging seas,
Fret not my child—with scars and all—I'll recognize you,

# "WEIRDNESS"

Follow me along this story of childhood memories,
Hey, did you have any childhood weirdness?
Let's share some things that appeared in the darkness,
Hold on—you'll in for a phenomenal awareness,

We lived in the projects—known as Loveman Village,
Back in the day—those were our townhouses—little villas,
It was like living in a three story penthouse—without pillars,
We didn't know it was for the poor—people didn't snigger,

I've seen things living in the projects—that will curl a Viking's beard,
No exaggerating, I've seen weird,
Check this out—a fat man and skinny man lurking in the closet,
I wanted to hit them with a lock in the sock—and say lights out,

But, the next night, I saw a foot hanging out the window,
Man—I woke my baby sister—and said let's blow,
Wow, it was some strange stuff in that room,
And, it had nothing to do with the Bible's upper room,

In the neighborhood, children played kick ball,
We didn't know about soccer ball,
And, a few blocks down were two sister witches,
They would cast a spell—if your ball landed in their bushes,

Listen, one day the ball landed in the witches' yard,
No one dared to retrieve it—they were smart,
But, I decided to get the ball,
And, the witches casted a lifelong spell—hear me yawl,

The witches spouted mumbo jumbo,
And, I broke in the wind running—like Rambo,
Feet don't fail me now—feet took wings—I flew up the stairs,
Yes, I needed some serious prayers,

# "A NEIGHBORHOOD DISAPPEARED"

It was a small place called Elyton,
That had a mixture of shotgun houses,
And, single dwelling—homeowner houses,
Just a small neighborhood with working families,

See, shotgun houses—you could stand at the front door,
And, look all the way to the back door,
During a time of segregation—this was our Wall Street,
Where the dwellers lived humble and free,

A community where all was just trying to survive,
Living to make ends meet—in order to stay alive,
There was a lady who sold Tee cakes,
And, another lady sold frozen cups,

Yep, the neighborhood had its own entrepreneurs,
Some were construction owners,
Don't forget the ones with janitorial services,
A neighborhood filled with thriving businesses,

We even had our own swimming pool,
Thanks to God's natural flood,
The rain reached above the pillars,
But, the floods didn't wash away the fixtures,

There were tornados, floods, and natural disasters,
They didn't destroy the neighborhood,
There were outsiders in gangs,
And, they didn't destroy the neighborhood,

The small community stood strong against the odds,
Because of the love in the hood,
Through all adversities—the community stood,
The politicians flatten the houses—greed destroyed a neighborhood,

# "SOULS DON'T DIE"

How do you know souls don't die?
Well, if you really want to know,
Come, follow me on the space shuttle--Challenger,
As this awakening will be a cliff hanger,
So, put on your gravity belt—don't dangle,

Now, we're not talking extra-terrestrial,
Or, things that are supernatural,
No, it's the experience of souls being unilateral,
Infused with one body—in an endless universe,
That's known as the mystical celestial,

Energy is not created nor destroyed,
So, the soul is immortal—it's created by God,
What's created cannot be destroyed,
God created Heaven and Earth—with a lightning rod,
As the story goes—the earth was dark and void,

Wrap your mind around this analogy,
At conception, the soul immortalized the body,
Yes, the soul and spirit are invisible and immortal,
Last breathe leaves—the invisible finds its portal,
The soul is like a person's teleportal,

Have you ever experienced Déjà vu?
When the soul recalls past memories—says guess who,
It's like putting the brain on steroids,
And, snapping pictures with Polaroids,
Then, the soul orbits the body like fast asteroids,

The soul can only reconnect by God's appointment,
To find its familiar host for encampment,
Yes, God controls the soul's assignment,
What God created has divine anointment,
Therefore, the soul is immortal—void of embroilment,

# "GOD'S JUSTICE IS NOT BLIND"

By society's standards, Lady Justice is blind,
But, we know that's not true—their lying,
Because the courts convict the innocent of crimes,
There's no moral equity—Lady Justice is not blind,

It's been said, justice deals with moral equity,
But, let me expound—iniquity isn't serenity,
Justice and righteousness are like synonyms,
God will judge the just and the unjust—His eyes aren't dim,

Didn't God say, vengeance is mine—I will repay,
Listen, to the cliché—every dog has his day,
Judgement day is coming—there's no delay,
God's justice is not blind—it's not far away,

Justice is who God is—I Am, that I Am
God's justice does not conform,
Because, God is infinite in His own self-existence,
And, He'll announce ones' sentences,

Hear ye, hear ye, here comes the judge,
The true and living God—might be persuaded to budge,
God is the judge of mercy and redemption,
Before dealing the penalty—God can grant exemption,

Man's judgment verses God's judgment—you can't compare,
With man—there's no forgiveness—so beware,
As gold is an element in itself—with no change,
So, God is God—His justice is prearranged,

God is the ultimate justice—in God we trust—He's not blind,
Can't you see the victorious saints being unbind?
Saints standing on the sea of glass—mingled with fire,
Yes, God sits on the judgement throne—saints don't despair,

# "LOOK WITHIN"

You've lived your whole life wanting love,
Looking for love in all the wrong places,
Thinking you could find it in a man,
Man has never been your biggest fan,

You ask yourself what you did wrong,
And, why so much abuse and pain,
All you ever wanted was to be loved like a queen,
Nothing more—nothing less, why men so mean,

Eye opener—you realize—love isn't found in a man,
Nor is love found in material wealth,
Can you hear that still small voice?
You've always had a choice,

Hear the voice—chose you this day who you will serve,
But, the voice is drowned out—by fleshly desires,
It's not too late—true love lives within,
Just allow your heart to listen again,

Aren't you tired of man's lies and false promises?
Creeping around from your bed to another,
Get some back bone—dump the bastard,
You know his bed action—don't cut the mustard,

Even Viagra—won't make him stand at attention,
So, stop putting yourself through humiliation,
While looking at that man's smirk grin,
You're better than that—love lives within,

It's not about the physical attraction,
It's not about looking at bank transactions,
It's about having an honest loving relationship,
And, realizing a man can't sail your ship,

# "STILLNESS"

I sat by the Pacific Ocean, and watched sea gulls fly,
I walked in the woods, and gazed upon green pastures,
I ran up and down country red dirt roads,
And, I plucked ripen pears out of the orchid,
Yes, this is where I found the stillness of God,

I lay in wait for the chickens to lay eggs,
I mixed leftovers and fed the hogs,
I broke the ground in rows, to plant seeds,
With, my long sack on my side, I picked cotton,
Yes, this is where I found the stillness of God,

I wrung chickens' necks and plucked their feathers,
I chopped wood to keep warm by the fire,
I pumped water from the pump—to drink and to bathe,
Then, I drank peach leaf juice to kill tape worms,
Yes, this is where I found the stillness of God,

I sat in the blistering fields, and ate watermelons,
I even chopped down sugar cane,
I played out in the front yard making dirt pies,
Wow, it was fun drinking coffee from a blow,
Yes, this is where I found the stillness of God,

I enjoyed riding the big yellow cheese bus to school,
I learned to read, write, and do math around a coal burning stove,
I loved going to Prairie Farm Elementary,
Yep, learning was fun in the country,
Yes, this is where I found the stillness of God,

Now, I long for those days,
Since moving to the city—of noise,
A city of crime and void of kindness,
Oh, why did I leave blissfulness in the county?
Now, I read Psalms 46:10—to find the stillness of God,

# "LIFE IS AN ART"

Let's work with this idea—life is an art—full of strokes,
It all depends on your brush strokes,
It's how you brush the paint on the blank canvas of life,
That produces an everlasting picture full of harmony—or strife,
You control the brush—reflect your life,

There are many hues to begin your artwork,
Life's like a rainbow of colors—lay the brickwork,
How you prepare your canvas will dictate your life,
So, prepare well, to avoid a jackknife,
Choices in life—can improve or destroy real life,

An artist eye—is like Moser's charm,
Not afraid to get started—set off your own alarms,
Your canvas maybe blank—don't fill encaged
Start brushing on colors—will eliminate the white page,
Color the canvas of life—build your acting stage,

The swirl of an art brush is like a winding roads,
It feels like you're on the yellow brick road,
So, keep traveling that proverbial road with a stroll,
Click your heels like—Dorothy in the Wizard of Oz,
You'll be home—untarnished,

That's right throw as many hues on the canvas,
There're no boundaries or barricades,
Go ahead—break the glass ceiling,
Erect your own monumental skyscraper building,
Be an architecture—draft blueprints of your beginning,

Now, choose a frame for your masterpiece,
You've endured life's brokenness,
And, earned a leading role on the stage—take your bows,
As your face radiate like colors of the rainbow,
You're beautiful—so glow,

# "DON'T GO"

I saw you in my dream this morning,
And, we played like we always do,
It was a beautiful sight to behold,
Oh, how that did warm my soul,

I have fun memories of us swimming—in Titusville pool,
And, you tried to beat the crap out of that boy,
For felling on me like a fool,
You sunk him like a buoy,

No, you didn't play that game—with the thugs,
Do you remember running my boyfriend across the tracks?
His long legs running like a Volkswagen bug,
It was your favorite past time—to set traps,

You always looked good—like men in GQ magazines,
I would always sneak and wear your sweaters,
They made my persona gleam like Vaseline,
With your sweaters—I made my own En Vogue adventure,

You bought me a yellow Easter dress with a stain bow,
A dress made of lace—for a Princess of the day,
Oh, how beautiful—a yellow like the rainbow,
That Easter—I remember it like yesterday,

I woke suddenly very distraught,
As the dream began to dissipate,
I cried out wanting to hold on with all my might,
Don't go—can you stay?

Now, you can only visit me in my dreams,
For, you had to take your deep sleep of rest,
I can't let go—if I do—tears will flow like a stream,
Don't go—our childhood days were the best,

# "DETOURS OF LIFE"

Sometimes life can throw you many fast balls,
And, you just can't seem to hit a home run at all,
You've gotten to the plate with your bat in hand,
Expecting to swing at the fast balls of life's demand,

But, you find yourself unable to make it to first base,
Because, of all the detour signs that pops in your face,
It's like being online checking your emails,
Ads keep popping up—you wish you had braille,

Finally, you realize those are the detours of life,
It's like throwing mud in your eye,
Designed to get you off your "A" game,
Fight for your rights to stay on the horizontal plane,

Never surrender, never give up, swing like Jackie Robinson,
Remember, he broke many barriers as a humanitarian,
Hold on—travel the roads not taken,
Then, search within for your awakening,

It's your time to shine like new money,
No more back roads, no more being the donkey,
You've discovered your pathway,
No more detours of life—you're flying high in the sky,

It's better than flying on Kitty Hawk,
God's given you an upgrade—a 747,
Now, fasten your seat belts—get ready for takeoff,
There's no more high turbulence—it's time for your payoff,

No more stressing over worldly desires,
No more succumbing to man's foolish lies,
No more planning your own route of escape,
Jesus is the truth and way—for Heaven's sake,

# "THE OVER RIDER"

You ever had a plan thrown a monkey wrench,
And, it appears that your life is on a pressing bench,
Is there a saboteur?
Yes, but there's an over rider,

Hey, you waiting to hear on a job interview,
Blockers and haters try to stop your debut,
Hang on in there—you'll erect a new venue,
The day has come to travel a new avenue,

Stop the struggling and midnight wailing,
Now, it's time to dance by the sky's twinkling,
You've paid your dues—to eradicate the blues,
The over rider has spoken—your haters didn't have a clue,

The forces meant you harm, like a tornado,
From the beginning, the Savior was your backhoe,
No weapon formed against you could grow,
Look at the over rider's power bellow,

The good book says, the righteous isn't forsaken,
Watch your enemies quiver like a defense formation,
Because the Savior executed an offense interference,
No need to call the kicker out—you've got a TD clearance,

Now, the angels are your cheerleaders,
Shouting your safety throughout the land like Paul Revere,
For, you have scored high—like a wide receiver,
Yes, you're protected by the over rider,

# "ARTIFICIAL TEARS"

Why artificial tears?
I thought everyone shed natural tears,
Tears of sorrow or tears of joy,
Aren't tears shed automatically?

Well, you would think that's true,
But, let me share a story with you,
Once upon a time, I knew a young girl,
She sang songs like a nightingale,

Songs that would warm anyone's heart,
That could make all troubles depart,
Never tears—just sweet melodies,
She was the little mahogany,

But, something changed her serenity,
That destroyed her world of solidarity,
And, shattered her imaginary Neverland,
No longer did the sweet voice sing in fairyland,

Years brought on an air of darkness,
Which surrounded her with harshness,
Then, the little Princess' world diminished,
Causing her life force to be extinguished,

She cried day and night—none stop,
If only she could call on Tinkle Bell—as her prop,
But, Tinkle Bell was too tiny,
So, the young girl called on the Almighty,

Father, Father, dry up the tears like a desert,
Let no more tears hurt your vessel,
Like fairy dust magic, tears ceased to flow,
Now, only artificial tears show,

# "GUARD YOUR HEART"

In this life there are so many pitfalls,
One would need a high-power telescope to see them all,
Contact NASA to borrow Space Shuttle Endeavour,
To zoom in to guard your heart forever,

Fake people seek to sink you with a battleship,
Always pretending to want a relationship,
But, mainly trying to block your progress,
So, you form a fortress around the ingress,

To guard your heart from incoming nonsense,
Go ahead, build the wall of defense,
You must become a survivor,
So, unplug from the synthesizer,

You've been surrounded by talking heads,
With one agenda—to get in your bed,
It's time to post your Sentinels,
No, you're not being temperamental,

Guard your heart against the creeps,
All your life they've made you weep,
Now, it's time to stand like bamboo,
And, dismantle the organized coup,

Take back your power from your naysayers,
For, you are the major player,
And, reset the dial on your big screen,
To guard your heart with a submarine,

Dismantle unwanted bystanders,
Standing around cheering for you to sink in quick sand,
It's your world—block them out with your marching band,
Don't you feel the seven archangels close at hand?

# "MY STORY IS NOT OVER"

My life's been attacked with a hurricane Katrina,
It's like debris swirling around in a trash arena,
I've been in the clutches of the storm,
Entangled in a fierce thunderstorm,

What's held me together is my faith,
Which has kept me glued from a fickle fate,
There's no incoming hot lava—just sweet morning dew,
I'm jumping like a kangaroo,

Hey, the trenches are dark—like in a combat zone,
Mortars flying over my head, like searching drones,
But, God dispatched a legion of His own,
His weaponry is Heavenly grown,

Oh, the prince of darkness set a mean trap,
Then, God created my own defense app,
With one original design—in mind,
God counteracted the explosive bomb mine,

Therefore, I escaped the diabolical annihilation,
Yes, there's a host of angels plotting my navigation,
Check out my personal rover,
Because, my story is not over,

One, two, three, all eyes on me,
Watch me reset my story,
No reruns like on TV,
I'm reinventing me,

Troubles thought they could punch my ticket,
But, I did a 360° pivot,
And, began to rewrite my own story,
Hear ye, hear ye, I decree—my story is not over,

# "CITIZENSHIP"

There are different nationalities,
That creates a variety of citizenships,
Some hail from Spain, France, and Switzerland,
And, Rome to the Great Netherlands,

Though these are countries of great status,
There's nothing like having God's citizenship,
Where there are mansions and many rooms,
No homelessness—no dust brooms,

You don't need a visa or a passport,
Nor worry about stations that deport,
You are welcome in the Throne Room,
Where the angels sing Hallelujah—joy blooms,

Listen to the trumpets sound your arrival,
And, announce the Bridegroom's survival,
Being in the presence of the Most High,
That's everlasting citizenship—you can't buy,

No excommunication—no round-up situation,
Just you and the Bridegroom's ongoing celebration,
As you travel through the Heavenly inner chambers,
You have permanent citizenship—with favors,

Waving bye-bye to earthly imprisoning clamor,
To embrace a blissful sanctuary of glamour,
What you say—Heavenly citizenship is greater,
It beats earthly round-ups at Southern Boarders,

And, no deportation on an unmarked ship,
You belong to God's citizenship,
Now, drop the chains of fear,
You're hidden under a new banner—my dear,

There's no need for a visa, passport or nationality,
There's no interrogation about ethnicity,
There's no alien country,
So, come join a citizenship—of milk and honey,

45

# "FAITH ACTIVATES GOD"

"Now faith is the substance of things hoped for."
I say by faith you can activate God's love.
Is faith the evidence of things not seen?
Yes. Love requires God to intervene.

"Love hides a multitude of sin."
It's by grace you can win.
Then, mercy quietly appeared.
So, by Grace and Mercy sin disappeared.

"Let not your heart be troubled."
Don't let anything burst your bubble.
Though, troubles knock and pound on your vessel.
Just remember God's love is transcendental.

"Rejoice not in iniquities, but rejoice in truth."
There in truth you'll find a break through.
Faith is the action that puts God in motion.
To show you favor above life's commotion.

"If you have faith as a grain of a mustard seed."
Look at the mountains that will recede.
You have the power to bind and erase evil off the chart.
Only by faith can you unlock God's heart.

"By whom we have access by faith."
It's like driving down a multi-lane interstate.
What a blessing being God's preference.
And, overcome tribulations to ignite hope and patience.

"For we walk by faith and not by sight."
Lest you stumble in the dark of night.
By faith you will activate God's eternal mercy and grace.
To live in the Father and the Son's warm embrace.

# "A FILL-IN"

Being the other woman isn't cool,
Just a fill-in on the weekend—twirling on a stool,
Or waiting by a phone—hoping it will ring,
Here's a reality tip—get a grip and see what life will bring,
Stop centering your life on a one-night fling,

You are better than that African Queen,
Recall your rich heritage and reclaim your self-esteem,
Remember, queens don't bow down,
Nor, be treated like a clown,
Hold your head up high with your golden crown,

Let your king adorn you with fine linens,
Pearls, gold, diamonds, 'til your lives intertwine,
Don't settle for less—knowing you are the best,
Learn to appreciate you on this life's quest,
For you are unique—not in a contest,

Hey, remember Betty Wright's song "Clean-Up Woman",
That's not you noblewoman,
You are chosen and set aside for greatness,
To soar like an eagle with grandeur and grace,
And, no worries of being a fill-in disgrace,

Oh, you heard the song by Homer Banks,
"If loving you is wrong, I don't want to be right",
Not cool—not tight—not bright,
Don't be a fill-in home wrecker,
Change the wiring in your circuit breaker,

# "CROSSING THE CENTURIES"

Love was loss in the 21st Century teleport,
As our souls traveled back and forth,
Through the cosmic celestial plane,
Our love could not withstand the heartache and pain,
That caused our love to slide down a faucet drain,

Our ships passed on the nightly sea,
But, we're too far apart, and cannot see,
Yes, our hearts sustained a deep bleeding crack,
And, our memories are fading like an obsolete 8 track,
No, we didn't get it right—and we can't backtrack,

While sailing nearby on the open dark sea,
It's like two comets breaking free,
We'll never reach the same dock,
We're like two empty ships sunk by cinder blocks,
Yes, we're in erythematic shock,

For, our love is like a pebble skipping across water,
And, never touching each other,
Ripples, ripples, in space and time—that's all we see,
The fog set in like a thick swam of bumble bees,
And, there's no lighthouse from the powers that be,

Our love has been torn from the foundation of time,
Eradicated from the eternal book and everyone's mind,
We're as driftwood from our own ships' wreck,
Oh, there's an albatross around our neck,
Our love will never cross centuries again—it's a tiny speck,

We're like two pirate ships passing in the night,
Looking for our loss treasure that's out of sight,
Now, time will not stand still for us to reunite,
No warm lingering embrace by candle light,
Centuries of our love destroyed overnight,

# "NO MORE BATTLES"

The battle was never yours—you picked up the sword,
All battles belong to the Lord,
Didn't you know it?
That's why you kept getting hit,

Calm down—take a break from the turbulence of life,
Go sit by the Pacific Ocean's bank—think of your afterlife,
And, watch seagulls overhead—in an easy flight,
It's time to stop the fight,

You've traveled this path of life with fortitude,
With a full breastplate of amour as a tool,
That shielded all your vulnerable emotions,
Now, it's time to check-out of all this commotion,

Look at the battles you fought,
How they left you very distraught,
And, no one stood guarding your back,
No doubt—that's a fact,

Now, put away your shield,
It's time that you yield,
To enjoy the golden latter years,
Safe from the battle field,

Take a walk on the sandy beach,
Pick up star fish under your feet,
Watch the sunset across the ocean shore,
No more battles knocking against your core,

# "UNKNOWN LOVER"

Have you ever had a dream of an unknown love?
Let's explore possibilities—it's like angles above,
Could it have been an angelical visitation?
To encounter a pure tender manifestation,

The encounter is better than having a billion,
It's like sitting in a field eating watermelon,
Savoring each juicy bit, that can't be beat,
This kind of love will turn up the heat,

The imaginary dream lover stirs your soul,
With surety, meekness, but yet strong and bold,
Your eyes sparkle like fireworks on the 4th of July,
Causing you to lose words—you become shy,

This unknown lover creases your face gently,
And, seals a soft kiss of serenity,
Then, gently lay your head upon his chest,
Embedding security—safety at its best,

No unwanted common foreplay,
No dragon or octopus to slay,
Just a respectful unknown lover on the scene,
You've got the green light—scream,

And, it's not an overweight lover in the house,
You've been asked to be his spouse,
What you say, what you say,
Shout yes today,

# "UNDER HIS SHADOW"

Under His Shadow where peace, love, and happiness reside,
And, throughout the universe He nurtures and provides,
He who abides under His Shadow shall live,
It's a shield against the great heat—under His will,

Let Him lay hands on you—to keep you still,
Even the shadow of His hands engulfs you in steel,
Lie quietly under His shadow with great delight,
Stay close and in His sight,

Many look for solitude in faraway places,
But, find only vanishing dry oasis,
Hey, tap the great rock for the babbling brook to spring,
All Hail to the one and only King of Kings,

His days are like a shadow for all eternity,
There's no day or night under the shadow of the Almighty,
Did you see how He conquered death's reign?
Now, The Almighty steer the rein,

Never let His Shadow flee,
Just walking side-by-side emanates glee,
All nations and tongues will confess,
There's a secret hiding place, under His shadow to rest,

Come one come all to the Most High,
Bring the weary, the tired, and the broken hearted to abide,
It's time to sound the alarm—trouble is overturned,
They that dwell under His Shadow shall return,

# "CREATE YOUR OWN"

Hey, sitting by the phone waiting for a call,
This's the 21ˢᵗ Century—send a text to all,
Let's hang out—not in the mall,
It's time to get out and have a ball,

You've been sitting around anticipating,
Just send out a text alert to your BFF,
Come on—let's start a new tradition,
How about skydiving?

So, what if the world can't accept your awesomeness,
You're a star that illuminate much brightness,
Pick your friends to understand your boldness,
Eradicate others' coldness,

Now, it's time to get back on the dating scene,
Don't let one flopped love define your dreams,
Be like Mr. Clean—wipe away the stain,
Or, better yet—get a love vaccine,

Tick-tock, your clock didn't stop,
What's up with this mental block?
You just need someone to dust your crop,
That'll send you to the hilltop,

Get out of that closet of anticipation,
And, create your own love connection,
Yes, step out on the wild side—of temptation,
While cruising on the shore of Jamaica,

Create your own Love Boat on the open sea,
Let your juices flow to the canapé,
Now, let your engine run full throatier,
Like sweet chili spices—that cause you to holler,

# "FREE SPIRIT"

Can love be bridled with the chains of society?
That can create lovers' anxiety,
Or, will love be unleashed to soar uncharted territories,
To break the scrutiny of societal laboratories,

Don't cage love—let it run free like wild stallions,
Out of control on the open plain,
Never extinguish love—or allow it to be bundled,
But, let it run free like King Kong in the jungle,

What's the double standard for men?
They cross the age barrier to get younger women,
While, older women are called cougars,
How about calling them seasoned tutors,

Let's bridge the gap between double standards,
What's good for the goose is good for the gander,
So, women it's okay to prowl,
But, be wise as an owl,

Women, be forewarned,
Don't cross the line,
Robbing the cradle—can get you jail time,
And, you'll be calling an attorney on your own dime,

Card the prospect before you stake a claim,
All untamed love is not fair game,
Watch your step out there in the love trap,
Before you even let it snap,

No discrimination in the untamed love game,
But, don't seek unwarranted fame,
Just leave the cradle robbing along,
And, you won't be in the wrong,

# "PORTRAIT OF LIFE"

On a blank canvas paint your portrait of life,
Take as many roads to find your true destiny,
And, carve out your unique identity,
As did the famous Michelangelo,
Dare to be an original,

Will you be among the greats and climb Mount Everest?
And, be in the Guinness Book—not as a tourist,
Or, sing a melody like Frank Sinatra,
You did it your way—paint your portrait,
Dare to be a pioneer,

Can you stand on the shoulders of Duke Ellington?
Or be an inventor like Edison,
How about the drummer known as Martin Luther King,
A fighter for civil rights—he was known in Beijing,
Dare to be a peacemaker,

Do you like space travel?
Be one of the first in Quantum teleportation,
There's room for another Erwin Schrodinger,
Bean up to plant Mars without a shuttle,
Dare to be phenomenon,

Will you explore the infinite possibilities?
Write, sing, dance, explore, and paint your portrait,
You don't need anyone's endorsement,
Carve out your place in history,
Dare to be a mystery,

# "POWER TO BE"

Here's a cliché: Knowledge is powerful,
Yes. But, love is beautiful,
For, love hides a multitude of faults,
Especially, when your soulmate defaults,

Really, does absence make the heart grow fonder?
Well, try it and see if your lover goes asunder,
Bussy-Rabutin said, absence is to love as wind is to fire,
Fan the flames, don't use an extinguisher,

Cars, houses, and material things you can possess,
But, there's no price on love—it's a valued asset,
Someone said, you don't have to give me money,
Love is free—just give it away—honey,

Don't force love—set it free,
And, if it's meant for you—love will come back,
Like a locomotive—on a fast Amtrak,
That' a fact,

The most profound love is loving yourself—you'll see,
Watch—you'll never be lonely—trust me,
Stop looking for love in all the wrong places,
Love will find you—among manikins in showcases,

Here's a riddle: What can't be seen or touched?
But, have an everlasting approach,
Give Helen Keller her props—let's record,
"The most beautiful things must be felt with the heart",

# "A TRIBUTE TO THE GREATEST"

Put your love on blast with surround sound,
Pump up the speakers—around town,
With a built-in system of stereophonics,
And, travel in time to the '70's with The Delfonics,
"La- La-La Means I Love You", it's exotic,

Check out the King of Pop,
MJ's—"The Way You Make Me Feel" causes one to drop,
This great hit—topped the chart,
With "You Are Not Alone"—MJ—you'll never depart,
I "Remember the Time"—MJ was the Jackson 5,

Let's hear from the R&B queen of soul,
Whitney Houston, "I Look To You",
Your music will never grow cold,
Yes, your fans "Will Always Love You",
Memories of you forever—so take your stroll,

A tribute to one of the greatest—Luther Vandross,
True love is forever—though you sang "Once Were Lovers",
When I "Think About You"—I weep,
If I could wake you from your sleep,
You could "Buy Me A Rose" that smells ever so sweet,

"In My Time" by Teddy Pendergrass reaches deep in my core,
This song causes all inhibitions to float out the door,
I'll be what he's been searching for,
Oh, "When Somebody Loves You Back" it's time to explore,
It's like a "Love T.K.O."—for sure,

"Purple Rain" leaves no pain says Prince the icon,
And, Hollywood didn't use you like a ping pong,
That's right—you said it, "You Don't Have to Be Rich",
You invited All into your world—even the snitch,
Here's a "Kiss" for you without a hitch,

# "A SOUL'S DESIRE"

I woke with you in my heart—burning like a forest fire,
I set a course in my time machine when we made each other perspire,
A time when our love was young, wild, and daring,
We were like buccaneers—nonconforming,

Recapping, when the window panes were foggy,
We wrote our names—with the sweat from our bodies,
Remember, we almost got caught,
Yes, thanks for the closet, where I let loose like a faucet,

This kind of love was meant to last a lifetime,
Our love was meant to be a <u>paradigm</u>,
We were young and foolishly in love,
Just a perfect fit like a hand in a glove,

Those courting dates are memorable,
Oh, if I recall—they were bearable,
We sat on the sofa—jammed between the family,
No room to get a kiss or a hug—no touching of the anatomy,

But, if the front porch could talk—that's another story,
You had me singing like a canary,
Hallelujah, Hallelujah, what fiery kissing,
It took me to the Eiffel Tower swinging,

What happened to our graveyard love?
Our forever dissipated in the thick grove,
We no longer walk side-by-side,
Or play by the roadside,

My soul's desire is to recapture our forever,
And, be suspended in my time machine peradventure,
Where we enjoy and recapture yesterday's ecstasy,
This is my heart's desire and fantasy,

# "THE OTHER WOOER"

You left the door unguarded—for an intruder,
After being temporally out of commission—entered a suitor,
A wooer stampeded in like a buffalo,
Seeking to graze on your unguarded waterloo,
The wooer tried to steal your boo,

Whoop,--there it is—your replacement staked a claim,
Another's throwback—becomes a wooer's hall of fame,
Now, you must count the cost of losing a crown jewel,
Who said life couldn't be cruel,
There's no pleading your case—before the tribunal,

It's like leaving the stable door ajar,
And, your prize Clydesdales escape under the crossbar,
'Causing you to wish upon a star,
For a second chance,
Before the wooer put your lover in a trance,

Be like Mike Tyson—take no punches,
Fight to the end—with counterpunches,
Don't think love is a free lunch,
Anything that's worth having is worth the fight,
Tell the wooer it's time to take flight,

Guess what—good news, it's time to advance,
In the eyes of the forgotten, sparks romance,
So, do a Greek show dance,
And, fall on one knee to present a ring,
Now, you'll jumping up and down on a box spring,

Serve notice—you've taken a permanent resident,
And, proclaim—get back Jack—this is not a hint,
Pull up your staked claim out of my Paradise,
Don't let me tell you twice,
No Trespassing—danger slippery ice,

# "GIVE LOVE A CHANCE"

I've been hiding in the background,
Just looking from afar—like a mute button with no sound,
Unable to display my love that's so profound,
This kind of love exist once in a lifetime,
How can I keep it hid—when it keeps me awake at bedtime?

Sometimes, I want to shout from the highest elevation,
And, proclaim this love to every nation,
I want to defy gravitation,
Without a space suit and float to a distant planet,
Or, maybe, I should go oceanic,

This love that I have cannot be harnessed,
Nor, will it ever be tarnished,
But, I'm faced with a dilemma,
If the world knew—I'll be hit with a tremor,
Can't broadcast my love with an antenna?

Silently, I hide in the shadow of despair,
In fear of never being able to share my heart,
If, only I knew how to fight what's keeping us apart,
But, we shuffle the conversation—not knowing where to start,
As Shakespeare said, "To thine own self be true"—let's be smart,

It doesn't matter who approves or disapprove,
I make no apologies—it's time to grove,
My love inside—needs no excuse—that's no lie,
I've something going off like fireworks on the 4th of July,
News flash—give this love a chance—it'll never die,

Enter my spider web of love for serenity,
I promise, you won't lose your identity,
Come, feel endless happiness for all eternity,
No fighting, no pressuring—just love supremacy,
Let's no longer live in denial—give love a chance,

# "TIME TO MOVE ON"

Stuck, can't find the strength to move on,
I've being going through a rough patch—on my own,
And, I need rescuing by something strong,
Any suggestions—I'm out here all alone,

Send an airplane—Lockheed SR-71 Blackbird,
The fastest aircraft to swirl me forward,
How about the space shuttle—Discovery—on the double,
To catapult me to Venus—away from my trouble,

Or, better yet—the helicopter--Black Hawk Huey,
I'm sending an SOS signal—someone sunk my buoy,
Can I get the Marines—the fighting machine? Yes, I can,
Let's twitter an alert: the Navy Seals rescue by air, sea, and land,

A tribute to Fontella Bass's "Rescue Me",
I'm in a thick fog, boo—just plow through,
I need some TLC—in my boo's bronze arms,
I'm sounding an MIA alarm,

Curtis Mayfield says, "Move On Up"—even with complications,
No, this world has never understood my motivations,
I've been interrogated—placed under a microscope,
Even had to balance life on a trapeze tight rope,

No more 70's, 80's, 90's, spooky drama,
I've upgraded to 24th Century panorama,
Call me the futuristic Diva under Singapore's Dome,
News flash, I've moved on—I've come into my own,

# "SUSTAINABLE LOVE"

Put your love to a test—could it survive a hailstorm?
Or, will the turbulence knock you off the platform?
If a great tsunami blew against your hidden dorm,
Will you tuck tail or stand true to form?

Choices bring challenges,
Has your love being tried with strange circumstances?
Let's give you a mental exam,
To determine if you'll be caught in a jam,

Here's the Lover's Questionnaire:
1. Do you make your lover lose their individuality?
2. Do you nag like a hag and cause a lover to check out of reality?
3. Have you been unfaithful— exploring other sexuality?

Oh, don't get it twisted—these aren't questions of insecurity,
Just checking out your relationship stability,
To see if there's a need for a house cleansing,
Or, call in a priest to do an exorcism,

Let's take a play book page from Jay-Z and Beyoncé,
They defied the norm, and created their own getaway,
They refused to be dictated to or conform,
Now, look at their solid love platform,

Shine the spotlight on Will and Jada,
They found each other in the early '90's,
The Fresh Prince of Bel-Air did a righty tightly,
Jada's not going anywhere—says Will the almighty,

Let's not forget women's heartthrob—Denzel,
When Denzel grace the silver screen—women's bells ring a ding-ding,
What can you say, Pauletta rung the bell—got the ring,
These couples don't have a crystal ball—just a sustainable love theme,

## TRUST—that's all…

# "UNMEASURABLE"

Name some things that can be measured,
Okay, let's start with the Customary Unit,
Units of Weight: pounds, ounces, and one ton,
Let's keep exploring—go on,

Did you need to take a break to catch your strength?
What about the Units of Length?
Starting with inches, feet, yard, mile—now you're witty,
Denver is known as the mile high city,

Now, let's focus on Capacity?
The smallest unit is an ounce—welcome to the academy,
My daughter's nickname is half-pint,
Then, there's quart, gallon, and pint,

The best of all the units—Time,
Here's a riddle: a stitch in time saves nine,
Can you stop Father Time—in the tower?
You don't have the power,

Well, here's another brain teaser,
What's an economical pleaser?
Philosophers say success gains happiness,
Take a snapshot of this:

# "EXCLUSIVE RIGHTS,

So, you've got dibbs on your man,
Is he controllable like paddy in your hand?
Now, my sisters really—come back to the light,
Are you looking for a World War III fight?

How do you know that you have exclusive rights?
A marriage license is just a piece of paper typed,
He took the vows at the altar—to love and cherish,
But, lately—the splendor of love has perished,

Take some notes in shorthand,
While you take Course 101--Keeping Your Man,
Do your homework—study—stop being spoon fed,
Then, you won't worry about a cold empty bed,

Sharing a few tips—no tricks,
Listen then—I'll be quick,
Compliment him to boost his self-esteem,
Look him dead in the eyes—and you'll reign supreme,

Want more of the bait and catch—study guide?
Give him space to enjoy his alone time—you'll some be a bride,
Ladies, be attentive, ditch the phone—don't be a creep,
Having exclusive rights—isn't cheap,

Last piece of wisdom,
Be thoughtful—turn-up your charisma,
When you get something for yourself,
Get something for him—resign self,

## Take love off a bookshelf,

# "A STRONG PRESENCE"

Tonight, I felt something tugging at my heart,
It caused me to pause, then, in my mind, I hit restart,
I kept it moving, but envisioned you lying across my breast,
Could it be that love has risen like the Phoenix —from its nest?

Just a small thought of your presence has begun a healing,
To an empty heart and stirred passionate feelings,
It feels like the joy of the first Christmas,
As children lie awake anticipating Hershey kisses,

It's like visions of sugar plums dancing in my head,
As I tenderly engulf you close in my bed,
Yes, I feel shock waves overwhelming my virtue,
But, this kind of passion must be nurtured,

There's no shame in enjoying the mysterious visitor,
Maybe, this is an old fling trying to re-enter,
Whatever, I'll just enjoy the intruder twice,
Though my heart belongs to another—at flight,

A songwriter once wrote, if you can't be with the one you love,
Love the one you're with—sent from above,
That's right—don't deny your love rights,
Open up your heart—enjoy the shock wave tonight,

No regrets tomorrow because of the sunlight,
From light comes darkest—from darkest comes light,
This outer body presence is a love bond,
Therefore, our hearts are woven strong like yarn,

# "HEREAFTER"

I don't know what awaits me on the other side,
But, I'm grateful that I'm still alive,
What's on the other side—no one knows for sure,
But, I do know the love ones asleep are near,

I feel their love reaching from beyond,
Watching, over me—though they can't respond,
Yet, finding ways to make their presence known,
By contacting me by dreams, breezes, and flying eagles —not by phone,

They just watch from afar with protective defenses,
And, come to my rescue when people become offensive,
It's like having ancestral guardian angels,
Yes, I have security from all angles,

A warning haters,
Stop presenting smiling faces—you're masqueraders,
I've got my own built-in central intelligence,
My big brothers are still running interference,

This I know for certain—love is eternal,
I don't see, hear or touch them—they still act paternal,
For my brothers' love for me is everlasting,
Their love is like computers interfacing,

When trouble comes knocking at my vessel,
Jr., Jerome, and Buddy Boy awaken from their nestle,
These brothers were like the Three Musketeers,
However, they were not French speakers,

My brothers' actions spoke louder than words,
If you encountered the 3 any day—they didn't need a sword,
Make sure wind is under your feet,
'Cause you'll feel defeat,

**Olé to Jr., Jerome, and Bubby Boy**

# "HIDDEN PLACES"

I've had a reoccurring dream of traveling through a house,
With rooms as plenty as grapes in a winepress to arouse,
And, a hidden attachment of more rooms of splendor,
I'm experiencing a serious mind bender,

It's like I'm traveling through the chambers of Heaven,
In the center there's a circular pit filled with sweet odors,
Then, there's a golden throne surrounded by flashing light,
Wow. I think to myself—did my soul take an express flight?

My soul has taken an exotic free trip,
Guess what--not from an astrotrip,
But, with all expenses paid in advance by Jesus,
I've been swished away exploring hidden places,

There's a great mystery concerning Stonehenge,
Let's share a secret unknown to men,

Can you see the rainbow dome overhead?
That's the firmament that separates earth from the Godhead,

The mysteries of the ages are revealed,
To only those with the God seal,
God is the Supreme Being,
Timing is everything,

# "MESSAGES FROM AFAR"

We're going on a journey when the world was young,
And, when man walked in the Garden singing songs,
The first man—not concerned about wearing clothes,
Just hanging out with his animal friends—in the groove,

Then, God decided to make man a woman,
Oh, that's the Big Bang—man's woes began,
Let's call for a serious re-mix—of clay bricks,
Can God get a do over—to fix this trick?

The fallen one installed a monkey wrench,
To always keep man and woman in a trench,
When he was hurled into darkness—a third bolted too,
They instrumented a diabolical plan against the two,

Jealousy and Revenge—they are kin,
But, the fallen one and the third won't win,
For the Trinity installed a fail safety switch,
Guaranteed to work—without a glitch,

Here's wisdom for those seeking,
There's more than 144,000 entering,
The Paradise expands throughout the universe,
There's no north, south, east or west—news alert,

Surprise, the Kingdom has no directions,
That's a manmade concoction,
NASA sends shuttles to discover other life,
Hers's one for you—there's always been an afterlife,

# "CAN'T TRAVEL BACKWARDS"

There's only three that I loved—in this lifetime,
They were the thieves in the night,
Those three stole my heart—from its stationary socket,
Each one of them kept me hidden in their pocket,

Once labeled young and naive,
That be me—no street sense—can you believe?
I didn't know how to play the game of non-sense,
Love tore down my common sense,

Let me reminisce of my first innocent love,
Well, some may say it was puppy love,
At eight years old—but he was easy on the eyes,
Especially, watching how his hair flies,

Oh, I recall the special trip to the classroom window,
Just to deliver and orange aide drink—my hero,
Then, one day the puppy lovers parted,
Never to see each other—then developed a faint heart,

Forty years passed before a reunion,
Then, fate stepped to the plate—with Holy Communion,
They finally found the greatest love of all eternity,
When they share their faith in the Almighty,

The Father took the reins with a perfect direction,
Now, they share memories about God's creation,
Though years tick away—they'll never be apart,
'Cause they're doing the work of the Lord,

# "PARTNERS FOR LIFE"

For once in a million lifetimes,
We've found unconditional love that binds,
No sexual involvement—just pure lovingkindness,
This kind of love will last for eons,
It's that kind of love that creates permanent blindness,

Hear no evil—see no evil—our love has no faults
God must've went into the Gulf of Soul's vault,
And, created a masterpiece of His love—that we sought,
Love's no longer a society buzz word—that can be bought,
What The Father created inside of us can't be taught,

Why did God create such purity?
He saw that our vessels would sustain eternity,
Two vessels that will not conform to earthly lust,
But, share a profound spiritual quest,
To present to the world God's best,

We've traveled this way before,
But, mankind acceptance was very poor,
It's like we've been in a continuous cycle,
Trying to show the world God's life cycle,
Love is God's essence—to prove it—call Michael,

We're partners for life created for a purpose,
Created in God's image to be a demonstration,
God's love is nestled inside of us to present to all nations,
We must be love in action,
Partners for life—as love practitioners,

# "NO IMAGINARY FRIEND"

News flash—God's not an imaginary friend,
He resides within,
I can feel Him blowing in the wind,
I can read His Word through the Bible's pen,
God's not an imaginary friend,

Read the Word—it's not a stage script,
I've established an everlasting relationship,
Now, I'm sailing in the celestial Mother ship,
Resting from the earthly troubles and bad trips,
God's not an imaginary friend—He'll never dip,

I'm taking pointers from T.D. Jakes' "Scared Love Songs"
I want a lover that sticks closer than a friend,
I want a lover by day—not just at night,
I need Jesus to be the lover of my soul—on this universal flight,
God's not an imaginary friend—His love is tight,

When my eyes grow dim and vital organs cease to work,
I want Jesus—no phony quirks,
I need Jesus to guide me through the eye of the needle,
The one who's the wheel in the middle of a wheel,
God's not an imaginary friend—His love is forged in steel,

I'm not in a dream,
This's a live stream,
Heaven's right here—on a high beam,
I feel the Father's Supreme Being,
God's not an imaginary friend—He is my bloodstream,

# CLOSING WORDS

I write with inspiration from on high. Every poem that has been penned
came from a place deep within my soul. I have tried to
recite the poems by memory, but to no avail.
That is how I know every poem comes from the Trinity.
I am God's Ambassador, I yield my all to God's Glory. Use me Lord.

Ambassador for Christ,

*Dr. Stephannie S. Huey*

# ABOUT THE AUTHOR

Stephannie Oditta Sigler Huey was born in Birmingham, Alabama. She was raised in a one parent home—by her mother with five siblings.

She always knew that she was different. At the age of five, Stephannie preached her first sermon from her little blue book, <u>Jesus of Nazareth</u>. And, after being on the battlefield for the Lord, she got sidetrack and started looking for love in all the empty places. She experienced great heartache—which she conveyed throughout this book.

But, she never lost her faith. She finally, made her way back into the loving arms of her Lover for Life—Jesus. Then, she took spiritual vows—as a nun would—and has been completely consumed in doing the will of the Father.

On at least three occasions, Stephannie had an outer body experience and visited Heaven. At the age of five, she walked through Heaven and saw the crystal streets and a multitude of people waving as she passed by.

At the age of eight, while living with her great aunt in Hardaways, Alabama, she often played in the woods. On one beautiful clear day, she was able to see angelical beings going up and down a ladder from Heaven. To this day, the scene is as vivid as the day she first saw the opening in the sky—which allowed her to see into Heaven.

A period from 1975-1987, Stephannie experienced some very turbulent times in life—two divorces that devastated her—both were very physically abusive—to the point that she just wanted to cash in the towel. But, one day Jesus came and hovered at the foot of her bed of affliction. That time—Heaven came to her.

In 1991, she was ordained during her fellowship with A.O.H Pratt City Church in Birmingham, Alabama by Pastor Elder Elvis May. Her first sermon was "What Is A Life Without A Stain?" That day, many conveyed that they were spiritually moved and blessed.

There were many more struggles. But, now she is focused on the positive things in life and the love of Jesus Christ. She is no longer looking for love—for true love always existed in the Holy Trinity. She found her Lover for Life—in Christ.

She and her daughter, Taneshia are co-founders of God's Holy Tabernacle Church—which was originally incorporated in Denver, Colorado in the early 90's. Stephannie is the pastor and Taneshia is the co-pastor. Now, when they relocated to Birmingham, they re-incorporated the church and opened two churches.

Now, when Taneshia went in the Army for six years, Stephannie still carried on in the ministry—opening up a daycare and a private school k-12. Then, Stephannie experienced a devastating loss of her oldest brother—which caused her to take a sabbatical leave from preaching. She closed up both churches—you can say that Stephannie walked away from the calling.

Upon relocating to Virginia—Stephannie and Taneshia have re-joined forces and are back on the battlefield for the Lord. There is yet more to come. They plan to reopen God's Holy Tabernacle Church.

# ANOTHER PHENOMENA BOOK

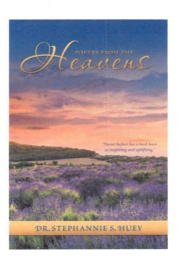

**Poetry from the Heavens: "Living Out Loud for Jesus"**
**Dr. Stephannie S. Huey**

Stephannie Huey has awakened the poet within her to share a compilation of lyrical verse that explores a variety of relatable issues that offer a glimpse into her faithful walk through life as she faced challenges, embraced joy, loved with all her heart, and suffered through heartache, with help from God.
Within her diverse poems, Huey reflects on the precious gifts of life: the spirit and soul, memories of days gone by, the bonds of sisterhood, the emotions that accompany of loving another, and the undying faith that comes with accepting Jesus into the heart. Throughout her collection, Huey shares a variety of lyrical styles that showcase her talent for digging deep into her own experiences to touch the souls of others and encourage self-reflection.

**ISBN: 978-1-4917-7728-2** (*sc*)
**ISBN: 978-1-4917-7727** (*e*) ● **76 pages**

# ANOTHER PHENOMENA BOOK

**LEGACY
OF
LIFE**

**"BRAVA"**

**DR. STEPHANNIE S. HUEY**
**Legacy of Life "Brava"**
**Dr. Stephannie S. Huey**

Dr. Huey, the best-selling author of *Poetry from the Heavens"*
*"Living Out Loud for Jesus",* is simultaneously publishing
*Legacy of Life "Brava"* and *Unsung Love.*
Both books are spiritually crafted by the Heavenly Father's inspiration.

• Available at Amazon.com, Kindle, and iUniverse Bookstore
• Visit our website at: www.iuniverse.com bookstore